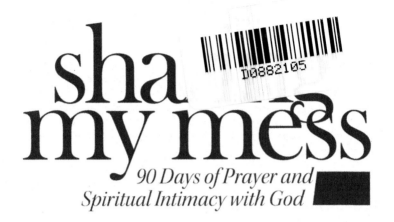

sha
my mess

90 Days of Prayer and
Spiritual Intimacy with God

Shani E. McIlwain

Be rich in the
fullness of God!

Love
Shani

purposely
created
PUBLISHING

Sharing My Mess
Copyright © 2015 Shani E. McIlwain

Scriptures marked NIV are taken from the Holy Bible, *New International Version*®, NIV®. Copyright © 1973, 1978, 1984, 2011 by Biblica, Inc.™. All rights reserved.

Scriptures marked NKJV are taken from the Holy Bible, *New King James Version*®, NKJV®. Copyright © 1982 by Thomas Nelson. All rights reserved.

Scriptures marked MSG are taken from the THE MESSAGE. Copyright © 1993, 1994, 1995, 1996, 2000, 2001, 2002 by Eugene H. Peterson. All rights reserved.

Scriptures marked GW are taken from the Holy Bible, *God's Word to the Nations.* Copyright © 1995 by Baker Publishing Group. All rights reserved.

Published by: Purposely Created Publishing Group™
Printed in the United States of America

ISBN-10: 1-942-83819-0
ISBN-13: 978-1-942-83819-7

This book is dedicated to the Best Mother Ever,
Patricia M. Kinard

&

My Precious Baby Girl
Alexia McIlwain

- - - - - - - - - -

table of contents

acknowledgements

Special thanks to:
My awesome husband Michael McIlwain.
My children Roderick, Raianna, Michayla, and Elisia.

Deloris B. Wood, Jeneane Becker, Emily Fair, Dene Chinn, Nicole Carr, Kennishia Shade, Veronica White, Jerrica McIlwain, Ronnie Harris, Rev. Theresa Brown, Nicole Brown, and Lillian Wise Wilson.

Pastor & First Lady Oliver & Pamelia Carter, No Limits Outreach Ministries, Audrey Cunningham, Natalie Richardson, Heather Schoonmaker, Dawn MacDonald, and Diane Geer.

Rev. Bernice Parker-Jones, Faith Presbyterian Church Emory United Methodist Church, The Williams Family, The Kinard Family, and The McIlwain Family.

foreword

By Pastor Bernice Parker-Jones

When I first met Shani about five years ago, I knew that there was an anointing on her life. The very first time I heard her sing, it was confirmed. What I did not know was that she was persevering through some very difficult times.

I met her shortly after the loss of her baby girl, Alexia. That was the proverbial straw that pushed her into writing this devotional. It had been deposited within her, but she had procrastinated in birthing it. This devotional is an outgrowth of the depth of pain and agony that Shani experienced and is her testimony of how God uses everything to His good. Throughout her journey, she found strength in the Word of God and is willing to share it with you.

It's not often that you find someone who is willing to open up their life to strangers; nevertheless, this is exactly what Shani has done in her book.

Sharing My Mess

Who we are today is a conglomeration of our past experiences—the good, the bad and the ugly.

Journaling these experiences has not only been cathartic for Shani, but the result offers hope to those who may question, "Why does a good God allow suffering?"

In the five years that I've known Shani and have served as her pastor, I am aware of many of the challenges she has faced. Nevertheless, she never lost faith. It seems that through it all, she learned to trust God more. Losing her daughter was perhaps the most challenging of all, and I believe this brought her back to the faith of her earlier years, the faith she saw in both her mother and grandmother. From this experience, we have a glimpse into her mess and how that "mess" was used to transform her life. Additionally, we see the faith that sustained her through a myriad of sleepless nights.

Often when we face great challenges in our life, we are tempted to run from God. On the contrary, Shani used her adversities to search God's Word for understanding. Like Rabbi Harold Kushner discovered along his journey in trying to make sense of his tragedy, Shani may not have gotten understanding and neither were her questions answered, but she discovered something greater—she recognized strength for the journey.

Shani E. McIlwain

In the pages of this devotional, Shani shares not only her mess, but more importantly, she invites us to the God who was with her as she traveled this journey. As you are traveling along this 90-day journey, and if you journal your thoughts while completing the exercises, you will be strengthened and will find hope.

During her season of grief and the writing of this devotional, I believe Shani shared one of the Apostle Paul's experiences. At one point in Paul's ministry, he sought God to relieve him of a "thorn in his flesh." The thorn was not removed, but he found something greater—the sufficiency of God's Grace. "My grace is enough; it's all you need. My strength comes into its own in your weakness" (2 Corinthians 12:9 - MSG).

As you follow the 90-day readings and searching the Scripture, you will discover a deeper relationship with God and will see your life being transformed. Likewise, as Shani discovered one of her varied gifts, so you may also do likewise. I am deeply humbled and grateful that Shani asked me to write this foreword. It is also an honor to be Shani's "Pastor Mom," and to witness her metamorphosis. This writing is just one of the many that God has deposited in her to share with us.

Shalom and Blessings,
Pastor Bernice Parker-Jones
Faith Presbyterian Church

opening

Sharing My Mess has been years in the making. I knew I was supposed to write, and I actually started a fictional novel about twelve years ago, but that thing we call "life" just took over. I became preoccupied with other things that I thought were important, but in reality, looking back on all the things that delayed this book, they were distractions. Distractions have a way of holding back your progress, but never God's plan. God uses the distractions of our lives to teach us and mold us into what He created us to be for His glory and His honor.

I am grateful for the distractions. With them came my mess—and in my mess, I grew up and grew closer with God. Through all the messiness of life, I am where I am supposed to be, right here, right now. I have humbly accepted my assignment to give to you a piece of myself that I feel is worth sharing. A piece of myself that glorifies and magnifies the God in me and will help transform you into who God has created you to be.

My transparency is not without some hesitation, but I know that my Father would not take me down a journey without His loving right arm of protection, and I am safe and secure with Him as my guiding light. To God be the Glory, now and forever more.

introduction

This 90-day journey into God's word is to help you build your personal relationship with Jesus Christ. It is in Him that we can do all things (Philippians 4:13), and as we build our lives around Christ as the center, we break open tremendous opportunities to become all that God has created us to be. We all know that we were created for a purpose, but sometimes we have a hard time grasping this idea because we live in the natural, when we should walk in the spirit, the Holy Spirit that Jesus left us with.

This guidance tool came out of a Bible study I did in my own church group. It was the study of Peter's walk on water and how learning to trust God can lead us to great things for God. Through that six-week experience, I learned so many things about myself, good and bad, that I will share with you over the next 90 days as we take some of my deepest issues and the scriptures that I studied to help me through some messy parts of my life.

I want this book to really help those who are new believers, but also remind all believers that transformation is an ongoing process.

You can be a follower of Christ for many, many years and know the clichés and the scriptures for points of reference, but do you have a relationship with Christ? Do you know Him for yourself? It is when we begin to examine our closeness with the Father that we fully understand and transform. Something clicks. It's like a lightbulb turns on for the first time when you really understand what a scripture means and why it is so important.

I can tell you all of my stories about those moments, but until you experience that for yourself, you will never fully come to the same understanding or appreciation I have. It is during those private, intimate moments with God that He reveals Himself to you.

It is my hope that as you take this journey with me, that you begin to transform and have a new appreciation for Jesus Christ, His ultimate sacrifice for your sin, and the everlasting love and favor He has for all of us. Let us begin the journey.

study & journal time

"The Spirit of the Almighty LORD is with me because the LORD has anointed me to deliver good news to humble people."

Isaiah 61:1 GW

MONTH 1

It All Starts with the Mind

I n Romans 12:2, Paul says that transformation starts with a renewing of our mind. We cannot keep doing things because society says it's right or because our friends and family are doing it. We must now work and do everything that pleases God.

The Message translation says it this way:

"So here's what I want you to do, God helping you: Take your everyday, ordinary life—your sleeping, eating, going-to-work, and walking-around life—and place it before God as an offering. Embracing what God does for you is the best thing you can do for Him. Don't become so well-adjusted to your culture that you fit into it without even thinking. Instead, fix your attention on God. You'll be changed from the inside out.

Readily recognize what he wants from you, and quickly respond to it. Unlike the culture around you, always dragging you down to its level of immaturity, God brings the best out of you, develops well-formed maturity in you."

Getting Your Mind Right

It is important to start out in prayer because it's the root and the nucleus of building your relationship. It is through prayer that you experience all that God is, so for the next 30 days as we focus on transforming our minds, our morning and evening prayer shall be:

Gracious and Heavenly Father,

I thank you for your grace and for your mercy. I humbly ask that you open my heart and mind to this study so that I can learn and grow from the words of your holy Bible. I ask that you remove anything from my heart that is not pleasing to you. Open me up to be a vessel for your glory. I thank you in advance for what you will do in my life. Transform me, Oh Lord. Transform me. Amen.

Life can certainly take us out of our routine to pray, or even try to convince us that we don't have time to pray, but in order to have any profound relationship with Our Lord and Savior Jesus Christ, we must make time with Him. Facebook—off. Twitter—off. Instagram—

Off. Texting – Off. Even our favorite television shows, or our favorite tele-evangelist cannot take God's rightful place on our schedules. When I first started writing this book, I didn't have time to fellowship with Him, and in my mess, it was revealed to me, why I was a mess to begin with.

Here's a blog post that I wrote during that time:

I am sharing my mess! I haven't written in a few weeks, because frankly I have been a MESS! I say that with such candor because it is the truth! I haven't stayed focused on Him; I haven't prayed nor studied the Word in completeness like I should. When I remove myself from all the connections that keep me in perfect peace, I literally become a MESS! I really do not have any excuse for my lackadaisical effort. I could place blame on lack of time, work, kids, husband, activities, the list goes on, but when I sit back and think about what I did have time for—well, I am not too proud of those things. I became restless, worrisome and irritable. I didn't have my words of encouragement that I share each morning on Facebook, and let's not get into my communication problem I experienced with my husband. I have been a complete mess!

5

But God! I love that conjunction! But: I was all these things for the past few weeks. *But God!* I called on Him to get me out of this busyness and just be still, and He answered me. He lets me rest in the meadow's grass and leads me by the quiet stream! But because of His grace, He did not scold me for losing my focus on Him; we picked right up where we left off. Because of His mercy, He has found favor in me when others did not. He makes me strong on the days I feel weak!

I am grateful to just be in His presence with another day to do His will. In this day and age of instant gratification, just take a moment to retreat. Experience the newness of spring. Find a trail to take a walk or a nice bike ride. Take the opportunity to just...be still. When you can be still for 10 minutes, minimum, oh the wonders of that communion with Him begins to unfold. He gives you peace and insight. He also shares the plans He has for you, but, again, you have to be still.

I am utterly amazed that in those three weeks of madness, I was learning to appreciate my still time. He teaches things to us when we are in the midst of things, and that's why all things work for good. He can use any situation in your life and turn into good for His glory, but we must remember that when we stray away from our prayer life, we can always come back because He is waiting for you; He already knows all about you.

What's your personal prayer? Write it here:

_____

_____

_____

_____

_____

_____

_____

_____

_____

_____

_____

_____

Week 1

For the first week, you will study:

1 Thessalonians 5:17-19
"Never stop praying. Whatever happens, give thanks, because it is God's will in Christ Jesus that you do this. Don't put out the Spirit's fire"

Pray continually, give thanks in all circumstances, for this is God's will for you in Jesus Christ. Talk to Him every morning, midday and night. It is important to establish a relationship with God that you can go to Him every hour. Ask Him to reveal Himself to you and give thanks for all things, good and bad.

It is important to thank Him for even the small things, because in doing so, we transform our minds, and our focus becomes more about honoring and celebrating the wondrous works of our Creator, rather than any problem we may be facing.

For the next seven days, think of one thing that you are thankful for. Focus on that one thing and expound on that during the morning, afternoon and evening. You can start with: Today, I am thankful for my job. Then find three things about your job for which you are thankful. Because we awake with brand new mercies every morning, we can find something new to be thankful for each and every day.

Thanking God for just the small miracles and mercies in your life increases your gratitude for Him. Imagine how you feel when you do something for someone and he/she doesn't say thank you. One of my biggest pet peeves is that my husband rarely says "Bless you" when I sneeze. I don't know why it bothers me so much, but, one day, when I got annoyed by the lack of manners, God reminded me that's how He often feels when we don't acknowledge Him.

There are times when we get so consumed by things that we don't put them in the right perspective or priority. Here I am getting mad at my husband when I haven't even given my best manners to my Savior. It's a humbling admission, but it helps us in so many ways, teaching us that we need to show as much grace to others as God gives to us. We learn that we all fall short, and we all have an opportunity to do better next time.

Giving God thanks for all things, in all situations, is a process that teaches us that He is really all that matters. In doing so, we're made more Christ-like.

Today I am thankful for _____
because:

1. _____

2. _____

3. _____

Today I talked to God about:

_____

_____

_____

_____

_____

_____

_____

_____

_____

Reflection

Today I am thankful for _____
because:

1. _____

2. _____

3. _____

Today I talked to God about:

_____

_____

_____

_____

_____

_____

_____

_____

Reflection

Today I am thankful for _____
because:

1. _____

2. _____

3. _____

Today I talked to God about:

_____

_____

_____

_____

_____

_____

_____

_____

Reflection

Today I am thankful for _____
because:

1. _____

2. _____

3. _____

Today I talked to God about:

_____

_____

_____

_____

_____

_____

_____

_____

Reflection

Today I am thankful for _____
because:

1. _____

2. _____

3. _____

Today I talked to God about:

Reflection

Today I am thankful for _____
because:

1. _____

2. _____

3. _____

Today I talked to God about:

_____

_____

_____

_____

_____

_____

_____

_____

Reflection

Month 1:   Week 1 - Day 7

Today I am thankful for _____
because:

1. _____

2. _____

3. _____

Today I talked to God about:

_____

_____

_____

_____

_____

_____

_____

Reflection

Intimidated By Prayer?

Sometimes we think we are doing everything right in regards to communicating with God. We ask for things, and when God doesn't answer us, we feel conflicted, rejected and disconnected with the Father. It is during these times that we have to be honest with ourselves.

Look in the mirror.

What are you asking for?

What are you doing aside from praying?

Yes, God wants us to live a victorious life, but we cannot just ask for things we want and not put in the work, so this week, we are going to focus on another scripture that will help us to start working.

Week 2

For the second week, you will study:

John 14:15
"If you love me, obey, my commandments."

This sounds like a simple task, but we all fall short on this. That is why we need the Holy Spirit to help us. We have to be obedient to the word of God, and He will certainly do what He promised. When you believe in Him, trust in Him, have faith in Him, love one another, and forgive each other, then you can see God move in your life and your prayers will be answered. You cannot stop praying because you are convinced God isn't listening. You have to continually seek Him, day in and day out.

The Old Testament is a reminder of how hard it was for God's chosen people to keep all the rules. They fell short over and over. That is why we need Jesus Christ, who saves us from ourselves. I was struggling with issues like unforgiveness, bitterness, resentment, and the list goes on, so I had to go through a process of learning how to release those things from my heart.

Little Things Hinder

Little things can separate us from the full experience of God's presence. Oftentimes, we look at the 10 commandments and say, "Well, I never did those things." One day, as I was preparing to write, I realized that I have broken every single commandment at one point in my life. Every first Sunday we recite the Prayer of Confession, and there is a part in there that struck me: "We acknowledge and confess our manifold sins; which we, from time to time, most grievously have committed by thought, word, and deed." Many times my thoughts are not Christian like. For instance, there were times in my first marriage that I thought about murder. I am so thankful that I never followed through on that act.

As I went down the list of the 10 commandments, I realized that I didn't always honor my mother, so I am clearly not squeaky clean of the commandments outlined by Moses. And let's not get into the sins we unknowingly commit. Saying we are going to do something and don't, hearing clear instruction from God and not obeying. This book isn't to bring anyone down, but transparency helps me release things that keep me from serving in my full capacity.

I sat there, realizing how messed up I am, yet how God still loves me and uses me. He even uses my mess. How incredible is that? That is something to make you just SHOUT! Little things, deep down inside the heart, way down deep, are blocking your experience. What about that little white lie you tell when you call out sick or the bag I hide in my car because I told my husband I didn't have any money. BUSTED! We aren't perfect, but Jesus is. I love that song, "Jesus Will." Of course, it's a remake of a James Cleveland classic, but one of the verses says, "Who makes me do right, when I would do wrong? Jesus will, Jesus will." We cannot do anything without Jesus because He makes us want to do right. I realize the more I walk with God, the more He reveals things about me that I need to fix. I can't move to the next step without transformation, love, grace and mercy.

Whatever issues you are struggling with that you can't let go—turn it over to Jesus.

Experience the full presence of God in a powerful way. Whatever vices you are facing, whatever is not pleasing to God, ask Him to remove from your heart. This week's journal lesson is to write down the messy things you did this week. Do not leave anything off the list, no matter how trivial you think it is. Even if you are embarrassed by it, God already knows what it is, so write it down.

Today I was messy with _____

_____

_____

_____

_____

_____

Today I talked to God about:

_____

_____

_____

_____

_____

_____

_____

Reflection

Today I was messy with _____

_____

_____

_____

_____

_____

Today I talked to God about:

_____

_____

_____

_____

_____

_____

_____

Reflection

Today I was messy with _____

_____

_____

_____

_____

_____

Today I talked to God about:

_____

_____

_____

_____

_____

_____

_____

Reflection

Today I was messy with _____

_____

_____

_____

_____

_____

Today I talked to God about:

_____

_____

_____

_____

_____

_____

_____

Reflection

Today I was messy with _____

_____

_____

_____

_____

_____

Today I talked to God about:

_____

_____

_____

_____

_____

_____

_____

Reflection

Today I was messy with _____

_____

_____

_____

_____

_____

Today I talked to God about:

_____

_____

_____

_____

_____

_____

_____

Reflection

_____

_____

_____

_____

_____

_____

_____

_____

_____

_____

_____

_____

_____

_____

Today I was messy with _____

_____

_____

_____

_____

_____

Today I talked to God about:

_____

_____

_____

_____

_____

_____

_____

Reflection

Week 3

For the third week, you will study:

Psalm 51:10-12

Create a clean heart in me, O God, and renew a faithful spirit within me. Do not force me away from your presence, and do not take your Holy Spirit from me. Restore the joy of your salvation to me, and provide me with a spirit of willing obedience.

If you completed Week 2's lesson, then I know you may be tired of writing. It's okay, but I am sure that through all those journal entries, you found some things you do that may have you feeling conflicted. Was there a day that you only prayed once, or not at all? Did you seek out Godly counsel? What did you do instead? It's alright because God gives us brand new mercies each day and another day to get it right. You will get there, one day at a time. Trust me, you will get there.

There are so many stories in the Bible where people who loved the Lord fell short. David was described as a man after God's own heart, having absolute faith in God. Early in his life, David knew that God was to be

45

trusted and obeyed. Like us, David sinned regularly, but always loved God and sought to repent for those sins.

This week's prayers should be of repentance. Ask God to forgive you for the sins that you committed. Ask Him to remove the iniquities that you thought may have gone away. Anything that you may be ashamed to admit, own up to it, and then give it to God in prayer.

Using your "Mess list" from last week, write a daily prayer of repentance from the mess.

You have to cleanse your heart of all things that are not of God. Your heart is His dwelling place, and He can't live inside a room that's a mess.

Lord, fix my heart from _____

_____

_____

_____

_____

_____

_____

_____

_____

_____

_____

_____

_____

Reflection

Lord, fix my heart from _____

_____

_____

_____

_____

_____

_____

_____

_____

_____

_____

_____

_____

_____

Reflection

Lord, fix my heart from _____

_____

_____

_____

_____

_____

_____

_____

_____

_____

_____

_____

_____

Reflection

Lord, fix my heart from _____

_____

_____

_____

_____

_____

_____

_____

_____

_____

_____

_____

_____

Reflection

Lord, fix my heart from _____

_____

_____

_____

_____

_____

_____

_____

_____

_____

_____

_____

_____

Reflection

Lord, fix my heart from _____

_____

_____

_____

_____

_____

_____

_____

_____

_____

_____

_____

_____

Reflection

Lord, fix my heart from _____

_____

_____

_____

_____

_____

_____

_____

_____

_____

_____

_____

_____

Reflection

Week 4

For the fourth week, you will study:

John 14:12 NTL
"I tell you the truth, anyone who believes in me will do the same works I have done, and even greater works, because I am going to be with the Father."

We have come to the end of our first 30 days together. I hope this process has begun something new in your spirit. I hope it is opening you up to the possibility of greater things yet to come. Sometimes we think that we cannot accomplish greatness or have an abundant life filled with love, peace, joy and hope, but Jesus came that we may have life and have it more abundantly (John 10:10). We have to remember this.

This is amazing! I have read John 14 many times, but it wasn't until I was fasting in preparation for this book that I was reminded by this scripture. I spent many days of procrastination thinking I wasn't ready or good enough to even write a book like this. When I first read this, it gave me so much power. If we believe in Jesus, we can do the same works He did—even greater. I am in awe of this promise. God gives us so many promises, but we are too scared to trust, believe, honor, fast, and pray. What is holding us back? What is holding you back? Is it fear? Is it self-esteem issues?

This week, write down one goal each day that you want to achieve for yourself, and the reasons why you haven't started to pursue them.

Do you want to go back to school?

Learn how to drive?

Learn a new language?

Start a ministry?

Get out of debt?

There is a burning passion inside you. What is it? And what is holding you back from beginning that task?

Goal: _____

_____

_____

I haven't started to pursue this goal because:

_____

_____

_____

Today I talked to God about:

_____

_____

_____

_____

_____

_____

Reflection

Goal: _____

_____

_____

I haven't started to pursue this goal because:

_____

_____

_____

Today I talked to God about:

_____

_____

_____

_____

_____

_____

Reflection

Goal: _____

_____

_____

I haven't started to pursue this goal because:

_____

_____

_____

Today I talked to God about:

_____

_____

_____

_____

_____

_____

Reflection

Goal: _____

_____

_____

I haven't started to pursue this goal because:

_____

_____

_____

Today I talked to God about:

_____

_____

_____

_____

_____

_____

Reflection

Goal: _____

_____

_____

I haven't started to pursue this goal because:

_____

_____

_____

Today I talked to God about:

_____

_____

_____

_____

_____

_____

Reflection

Goal: _____

_____

_____

I haven't started to pursue this goal because:

_____

_____

_____

Today I talked to God about:

_____

_____

_____

_____

_____

_____

Reflection

Goal: _____

_____

_____

I haven't started to pursue this goal because:

_____

_____

_____

Today I talked to God about:

_____

_____

_____

_____

_____

_____

Reflection

_____

_____

_____

_____

_____

_____

_____

_____

_____

_____

_____

_____

_____

MONTH 2

He is Everything and in Everything

I t never ceases to amaze me how He puts things in perspective for us in the blink of a second. Each day I get closer to him, God reveals His ways to me, and I am constantly reminded that He is EVERYTHING and controls EVERYTHING!

There was a polar vortex that came over the Northeastern region, and the temperatures were a record-breaking cold. I had to pump gas one evening, and within seven minutes, I was humbled. Now, I thought I had many prior experiences where Jesus entered my heart and I quickly humbled myself, but standing outside in that cold weather for seven minutes while I pumped gas made me feel so blessed to have the things I had. Things like gloves, a hat, a coat, clothing, and even a car that makes funny noises and is too small for my family of six. Nonetheless, I was so happy to have this car!

I was so grateful that God entrusted me with all these things. I was driving home to shelter and thought about those who couldn't do that; I wondered who they were and where they might be. Slowly the trivial things in my life didn't matter much, and I began to praise Him more.

This month, we will focus on SEEKING and why it is so important to seek Him and trust Him.

Week 1

For the first week, you will study:

Matthew 6:33
*"But seek ye first the kingdom of God,
and his righteousness; and all these things
shall be added unto you." KJV*

It was during a period of financial strains and an employment crisis that I fully embraced this verse. I encourage you to read several verses before the 33rd because, ultimately, we don't need to worry about anything else except seeking God. It may seem like a radical and a nonsensical thing to do, but it comes down to trusting that Jesus is the provider of all things. He has the capacity to take care of everything and our job; the only thing we have to do is seek Him.

During my moments of despair, wondering how the rent was going to get paid or how I was going to avoid the lights being turned off, I asked God to show me the hard truths about myself, my spending, and my waste. I asked God for a breakthrough with my husband and so many things. Hardships in our lives seem to be when

God is teaching us the most, or it could be that when we don't have anything else to rely on, we are open to hearing from Him more. Spend this week seeking God out as if He was in the flesh, right here next to you at work, sitting at your dinner table, or riding in the passenger seat of your car. You can do this through prayer and reading scripture. Take a few moments to stay focused on Him, consulting Him in everything you do.

Almighty and Gracious Father,

I humbly seek your face day in and day out. I want to be in sweet communion with you, loving you, praising your name, and magnifying your word. Help me in all things today and every day. Help me to stay focused on you and your word that never changes. This is my prayer in Jesus name, Amen!

While staying focused on seeking God in all things, use these two questions to journal:

1. What did you do this week that caused you to seek Him?

2. What obstacles and distractions did you have to overcome in order to fulfill this exercise?

I seeked God today because:

_____

_____

_____

_____

_____

_____

The obstacle or distraction I had to overcome was:

_____

_____

_____

_____

_____

_____

Reflection

I seeked God today because:

_____

_____

_____

_____

_____

_____

The obstacle or distraction I had to overcome was:

_____

_____

_____

_____

_____

_____

Reflection

I seeked God today because:

_____

_____

_____

_____

_____

_____

The obstacle or distraction I had to overcome was:

_____

_____

_____

_____

_____

_____

Reflection

I seeked God today because:

_____

_____

_____

_____

_____

_____

The obstacle or distraction I had to overcome was:

_____

_____

_____

_____

_____

_____

Reflection

I seeked God today because:

_____

_____

_____

_____

_____

_____

The obstacle or distraction I had to overcome was:

_____

_____

_____

_____

_____

_____

Reflection

I seeked God today because:

_____

_____

_____

_____

_____

_____

The obstacle or distraction I had to overcome was:

_____

_____

_____

_____

_____

_____

Reflection

I seeked God today because:

_____

_____

_____

_____

_____

_____

The obstacle or distraction I had to overcome was:

_____

_____

_____

_____

_____

_____

Reflection

Week 2

For the second week, you will study:

1 Chronicles 16:9-14

"Sing to him; yes, sing his praises. Tell everyone about his wonderful deeds. Exult in his holy name; rejoice, you who worship the LORD. Search for the LORD and for his strength; continually seek him"

Search for the Lord and for His strength. We don't have to do any of this by our own strength. In fact, we aren't capable of it. I am sure you had some obstacles last week trying to seek Him and stay focused on Him. If you didn't, that is awesome, but I humbly admit that I often fall short in losing focus on Him.

Thankfully, as the Apostle Paul states, His grace is sufficient in my weakness. So we can rest assured that when we need strength, He is able to provide it. Using your list from last week on the obstacles and distractions you had, ask God to give you strength to overcome them, or to teach you how to move past them.

As a Christian, you will have bad times, you will have obstacles; it is all part of a growth process. Embrace those things to help you get closer to the One who can take it and make it work for good. You are not in this alone.

Using your list from last week, write a quick prayer to help you remove the obstacles you are facing.

Lord, help me remove _____

_____

_____

_____

_____

_____

_____

_____

_____

_____

_____

_____

_____

_____

_____

Reflection

Lord, help me remove _____

_____

_____

_____

_____

_____

_____

_____

_____

_____

_____

_____

_____

Reflection

Lord, help me remove _____

_____

_____

_____

_____

_____

_____

_____

_____

_____

_____

_____

_____

_____

Reflection

Lord, help me remove _____

_____

_____

_____

_____

_____

_____

_____

_____

_____

_____

_____

Reflection

Lord, help me remove _____

_____

_____

_____

_____

_____

_____

_____

_____

_____

_____

_____

Reflection

Lord, help me remove _____

_____

_____

_____

_____

_____

_____

_____

_____

_____

_____

_____

_____

Reflection

Lord, help me remove _____

_____

_____

_____

_____

_____

_____

_____

_____

_____

_____

_____

_____

Reflection

Week 3

For the third week, you will study:

Psalm 27:8
"When You said, "Seek My face,"
My heart said to You, "Your face, Lord, I will seek."

David, the author of Psalms, was as the Bible describes, "A man after God's own heart." Among all of his great deeds, David also made a lot of bad decisions. Through all of David's sins and shortcomings, he had absolute faith in God. He knew he couldn't do anything without Him.

While this study isn't about David's life, I recommend that you take time to learn more about him and how his faith grew through his struggles and how thankful he was to God for His forgiveness as well as His wrath when he didn't obey. We can learn from our mistakes and find ways to honor God through all of life's situations.

During this week, write down each tasks you did that honored God.

Today I honored God by _____

_____

_____

_____

_____

Today I also talked to God about:

_____

_____

_____

_____

_____

_____

_____

_____

Reflection

Today I honored God by _____

_____

_____

_____

_____

Today I also talked to God about:

_____

_____

_____

_____

_____

_____

_____

_____

Reflection

Today I honored God by _____

_____

_____

_____

_____

Today I also talked to God about:

_____

_____

_____

_____

_____

_____

_____

_____

Reflection

Today I honored God by _____

_____

_____

_____

_____

Today I also talked to God about:

_____

_____

_____

_____

_____

_____

_____

_____

Reflection

Today I honored God by _____

_____

_____

_____

_____

Today I also talked to God about:

_____

_____

_____

_____

_____

_____

_____

_____

Reflection

Today I honored God by _____

_____

_____

_____

_____

Today I also talked to God about:

_____

_____

_____

_____

_____

_____

_____

Reflection

Today I honored God by _____

_____

_____

_____

_____

Today I also talked to God about:

_____

_____

_____

_____

_____

_____

_____

Reflection

Week 4

For the fourth week, you will study:

Psalm 11:7 NLT
"For the righteous LORD loves justice.
The virtuous will see his face"

Our ultimate goal while we are here on this earth is to see His face one day. We want to kneel at His feet. Spend some quiet time thinking about what you will do when you get to see Jesus.

Can you envision that encounter with Jesus?

How will you feel?

What will you say?

Take the opportunity this week to write down those feelings.

If I saw Jesus, I would _____

_____

_____

_____

_____

_____

_____

_____

_____

_____

_____

_____

_____

_____

Reflection

If I saw Jesus, I would _____

_____

_____

_____

_____

_____

_____

_____

_____

_____

_____

_____

_____

Reflection

If I saw Jesus, I would _____

_____

_____

_____

_____

_____

_____

_____

_____

_____

_____

_____

_____

_____

Reflection

If I saw Jesus, I would _____

_____

_____

_____

_____

_____

_____

_____

_____

_____

_____

_____

_____

Reflection

If I saw Jesus, I would _____

_____

_____

_____

_____

_____

_____

_____

_____

_____

_____

_____

_____

Reflection

If I saw Jesus, I would _____

_____

_____

_____

_____

_____

_____

_____

_____

_____

_____

_____

_____

_____

Reflection

If I saw Jesus, I would _____

_____

Reflection

MONTH 3

Fight for Your Faith

I t is my hope that at this point of the devotional, you are transforming. This journey with Christ and being a Christian is relational. You have to establish an unshakable faith and trust in God so that you can become a true disciple.

Believers—say.

Disciples—do.

While you are developing a personal relationship, you must tell others about how God is working in your life. It is important to remember who gets the glory. God will always find ways to remind us of that.

If we don't have reminders, we will begin to think that we have done everything by our own power, and that is simply not the case.

In this last month, find a partner to share this exciting transformation time with you. It should be someone you are comfortable with, and someone who can help you when you have questions. If you have a church home, ask your prayer partner or nurturer. If you don't have a church home, ask a friend who is a believer. Jesus often sent the disciples out in pairs, not just to testify about what great things He did, but to also witness to other people (Mark 6:7 – 13). Sharing your experience with someone you know is going to help you share your faith with strangers.

"Without faith it is impossible to please God"
Hebrews 11:6

Over the years, I have struggled with wavering faith. It was hard to put my complete trust in God. Even still, with all I have been through and all He has brought me out of, I have temporary lapses of unwavering faith. In 2014, my faith was tested to the utmost when I lost my job after 12 years. The same week, my husband was diagnosed with kidney failure and was told he would have to go on dialysis three times a week. We lived check to check and were already behind in most of our bills, most importantly our rent. To say it was a stressful period in our lives and marriage would be an understatement, but during this time, I learned that I had strong faith. I realized that I could not depend on a job more than I depend on God. I also realized that my help comes from no other place than the Father Almighty.

In those uncertain days, I was writing this book as well as preparing to teach my first Bible study. We were asked to do a character study on someone of obscurity in the Bible, but had a direct or indirect lineage to Christ. I can't honestly remember the moment I picked James, which leads me to believe it had to be the Holy Spirit's guidance. The book of James is a short letter to the religious leaders—Jewish Christians of that era. James reminds them of how utterly important it is to keep your faith at all times.

Accepting Christ as your Lord and Savior will not rid you of problems. Again, you will be tested, tried and tempted. There will be trials and tribulations in your life, but it is your faith and how you respond to all those things that will set you apart from others.

Salvation is free to all who accept Jesus Christ. While you don't have to do anything to earn salvation, you must live your life in such a way that everyone sees Jesus through you.

Week 1

For the first week, you will study:

James 1:2
"Count it all joy"

It is all about your perception. If you take account all the good with ALL the bad, and you "count," or consider it, take into account, add it all up, you will look at your situation as a test. Think about each situation you have been faced with and think how God brought you out of it.

When I wrote down every bad situation I have ever experienced, even when I was disobedient, I saw how God restored and protected me.

This week, recite this prayer:

Gracious and Heavenly Father, I come today giving you all the glory and honor. I count it all joy for the trials and tribulations of my life for I know that you are with me. I know that this experience is teaching me and testing me to be more faithful to you.

I put my trust in you. God, you are my rock, my sword and shield. You know all about me. Please help me to see things from your perspective. Help me to understand that this time in my life is to help me, not harm me. In Jesus' Name, Amen.

Write down each life experience that was a test (i.e., job loss, divorce, eviction, etc.). Write at least two tests for each day, and share your list with your partner.

Month 3:   Week 1 - Day 1

I've been tested with:

1. _____

2. _____

Today I talked to God about:

_____

_____

_____

_____

_____

_____

_____

_____

_____

Reflection

I've been tested with:

1. _____

2. _____

Today I talked to God about:

_____

_____

_____

_____

_____

_____

_____

_____

_____

_____

Reflection

I've been tested with:

1. _____

2. _____

Today I talked to God about:

_____

_____

_____

_____

_____

_____

_____

_____

_____

_____

Reflection

I've been tested with:

1. _____

2. _____

Today I talked to God about:

_____

_____

_____

_____

_____

_____

_____

_____

_____

_____

Reflection

I've been tested with:

1. _____

2. _____

Today I talked to God about:

_____

_____

_____

_____

_____

_____

_____

_____

_____

_____

Reflection

I've been tested with:

1. _____

2. _____

Today I talked to God about:

_____

_____

_____

_____

_____

_____

_____

_____

_____

Reflection

I've been tested with:

1. _____

2. _____

Today I talked to God about:

_____

_____

_____

_____

_____

_____

_____

_____

_____

Reflection

I've been tested with:

1. _____

2. _____

Today I talked to God about:

_____

_____

_____

_____

_____

_____

_____

_____

_____

_____

Reflection

Week 2

For the second week, you will study:

Ephesians 5:20
*"And give thanks for everything to God the Father
in the name of our Lord Jesus Christ"*

Be thankful. I am sure last week's exercise gave you many reasons to be thankful. Look at all the things God has delivered you from. It should also help you to realize that with each test, God has a proven track record. He isn't going to leave you or let you down. That should be something to shout about! Isn't this an awesome promise?

It is important to give thanks and have an expression of appreciation for God because it keeps our hearts in the right place. God commands us throughout scripture to be thankful. Having gratitude at all times helps us to not be bitter, especially through trying times. Thankfulness and bitterness cannot co-exist in the same heart.

Find three scriptures about thankfulness, and choose one to be your memory verse. We used this scripture at the beginning of our journey, and it is one of my favorites: 1 Thessalonians 5:18: *"In everything give thanks; for this is God's will for you in Christ Jesus."*

Hint: the Book of Psalms has several verses on thanks.

Scripture 1:

_____

_____

Scripture 2:

_____

_____

Scripture 3:

_____

_____

Using your list from last week, each day write about something you are thankful God delivered you from.

I am thankful that God brought me out of:

_____

_____

_____

_____

_____

Today I talked to God about:

_____

_____

_____

_____

_____

_____

_____

Reflection

I am thankful that God brought me out of:

_____

_____

_____

_____

_____

Today I talked to God about:

_____

_____

_____

_____

_____

_____

_____

Reflection

I am thankful that God brought me out of:

_____

_____

_____

_____

_____

Today I talked to God about:

_____

_____

_____

_____

_____

_____

_____

Reflection

I am thankful that God brought me out of:

_____

_____

_____

_____

_____

Today I talked to God about:

_____

_____

_____

_____

_____

_____

_____

Reflection

I am thankful that God brought me out of:

_____

_____

_____

_____

_____

Today I talked to God about:

_____

_____

_____

_____

_____

_____

_____

_____

Reflection

I am thankful that God brought me out of:

_____

_____

_____

_____

_____

Today I talked to God about:

_____

_____

_____

_____

_____

_____

_____

_____

Reflection

I am thankful that God brought me out of:

_____

_____

_____

_____

_____

Today I talked to God about:

_____

_____

_____

_____

_____

_____

_____

Reflection

Week 3

For the third week, you will study:

Hebrews 11:1
"Now faith is the substance of things hoped for, the evidence of things not seen"

Faith is a muscle that must be worked out. You don't need faith for things you can see. The Bible tells us that, "Now faith is the substance of things hoped for, the evidence of things not seen" Hebrews 11:1. When we see it is raining outside, we bring an umbrella to cover us. We don't need faith to believe that the umbrella is going to keep us dry.

We need faith that when we are faced with storms of life, God is going to keep us dry. We need faith that when we come out of the storm, we will share our experience with others and continue to give God the Glory He deserves.

It is that faith that God truly loves. He is extremely pleased when we share our faith in our talk, so this week, share your faith with others.

If you only feel comfortable sharing it with your partner, that's fine, but begin to share your faith with others as well.

Today I used my faith by:

_____

_____

_____

_____

Today I talked to God about:

_____

_____

_____

_____

_____

_____

_____

Reflection

Today I used my faith by:

_____

_____

_____

_____

Today I talked to God about:

_____

_____

_____

_____

_____

_____

_____

Reflection

Month 3:   Week 3 - Day 3

Today I used my faith by:

_____

_____

_____

_____

Today I talked to God about:

_____

_____

_____

_____

_____

_____

_____

Reflection

Today I used my faith by:

_____

_____

_____

_____

Today I talked to God about:

_____

_____

_____

_____

_____

_____

_____

Reflection

Today I used my faith by:

_____

_____

_____

_____

Today I talked to God about:

_____

_____

_____

_____

_____

_____

_____

_____

Reflection

Today I used my faith by:

_____

_____

_____

_____

Today I talked to God about:

_____

_____

_____

_____

_____

_____

_____

_____

Reflection

Today I used my faith by:

_____

_____

_____

_____

Today I talked to God about:

_____

_____

_____

_____

_____

_____

_____

_____

Reflection

Week 4

For the fourth week, you will study:

James 5:16b (amplified)
"The earnest (heartfelt, continued) prayer
of a righteous man makes tremendous power
available [dynamic in its working]"

You have made it! This is your last week of the 90-day study. Note, however, that transformation from the inside out is a constant process. This was just the beginning of what should be a consistent study of God's word. It is always necessary that you search the scriptures to find truth. I am just a vessel on assignment to help convey God's love and promise to all those who believe, who want to believe, and who may be searching. I am just a servant, who after years of disobedience and procrastination, finally said YES.

Remember that God loves you. Jesus died for you because He only wants the best for you. During this last week, continue to stay in prayer as it is your connection with God. You must have an active prayer life in order to have an active relationship with Jesus.

Everything, not some things, but *everything* should be taken to God in prayer. He already knows everything about you, so the great thing is you don't have to put on a show or use big words; just be the person God created.

Pray. There is power in prayer. James 5:16b (amplified): *"The earnest (heartfelt, continued) prayer of a righteous man makes tremendous power available [dynamic in its working]."*

As we come to the end of this transformation process, it is important to know that this is just the beginning. Every day is an opportunity to see things in a new way. Transformation is a constant renewing of your mind and doesn't end with this Bible study.

Prayer is a must. I can't do anything without prayer and meditation with my Lord and Savior Jesus Christ.

Thankfulness is a must. Being forever grateful for all things keeps us humble and mindful that we need Jesus for everything.

Faithfulness is a must. Without faith, it is impossible to please God. Faith is who we are as believers. It's the catalyst of everything we stand for and why we do things we do. We must have faith that God can do everything and anything.

When we stir all these things up—***prayer, thankfulness, and faithfulness***—we feel the love of Jesus wrap us up and protect us. It is because of that love that I can share myself with you and help you discover how much He loves you too.

Go. Share. Serve.

"God has made us what we are. He has created us in Christ Jesus to live lives filled with good works that he has prepared for us to do" (Ephesians 2:10 GW translation).

During this last week, write down your prayer for thankfulness and faithfulness. This will help you be accountable and consistent.

Don't give up! If you miss a day, just pray.

Today I prayed for:

_____

_____

_____

_____

I am thankful for:

_____

_____

_____

_____

I am thankful for:

_____

_____

_____

_____

Reflection

Today I prayed for:

_____

_____

_____

_____

I am thankful for:

_____

_____

_____

_____

I am thankful for:

_____

_____

_____

_____

Reflection

Today I prayed for:

_____

_____

_____

_____

I am thankful for:

_____

_____

_____

_____

I am thankful for:

_____

_____

_____

_____

Reflection

Month 3:   Week 4 - Day 4

Today I prayed for:

_____

_____

_____

_____

I am thankful for:

_____

_____

_____

_____

I am thankful for:

_____

_____

_____

_____

Reflection

Today I prayed for:

_____

_____

_____

_____

I am thankful for:

_____

_____

_____

_____

I am thankful for:

_____

_____

_____

_____

Reflection

Month 3:   Week 4 - Day 6

Today I prayed for:

_____

_____

_____

_____

I am thankful for:

_____

_____

_____

_____

I am thankful for:

_____

_____

_____

_____

Reflection

Month 3:   Week 4 - Day 7

Today I prayed for:

_____

_____

_____

_____

I am thankful for:

_____

_____

_____

_____

I am thankful for:

_____

_____

_____

_____

Reflection

about shani mcilwain

Shani McIlwain was born in Los Angeles in the Queen of Angels Hospital. In 1982, she and her mother moved to Hancock, New York. While there, she learned to play the violin, played sports, studied scripture, and adopted her love her writing. After high school, she went to Hampton University where she majored in History Education.

After college, she moved to DC, delivered her son, got married, had a daughter, and then divorced. Not long after, she lost her mother, birthed another daughter, and then twin girls, one of whom passed away. She later remarried, found work as a Quality and Business Process Manager, joined a church, and began her journey of healing through spirituality, love and writing.

In the middle of her mess, she realized that Jesus is real. "He's more than a song. He's bigger than anything and everything I could imagine, and I wholeheartedly believe that my calling is to empower others to get know Jesus in a way that will transform their lives."

She enjoys writing, teaching, storytelling, speaking, giving back to the community, spending time with her family, and having fun! For more information, be sure to visit www.ShanimcIlwain.com.

WE WANT TO HEAR FROM YOU!!!

If this book has made a difference in your life Shani would be delighted to hear about it.

Leave a review on Amazon.com!

BOOK SHANI TO SPEAK AT YOUR NEXT EVENT!

Send an email to booking@publishyourgift.com

Learn more about Shani at
www.ShaniMcIlwain.com

- - - - - - -

FOLLOW SHANI ON SOCIAL MEDIA

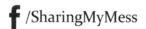 /SharingMyMess

CPSIA information can be obtained
at www.ICGtesting.com
Printed in the USA
`SOW03n1812180916
54FS